ARMED SERVICES

Jim Brush

EDGE
FRANKLIN WATTS
W
LONDON·SYDNEY

First published in 2010 by
Franklin Watts
338 Euston Road
London NW1 3BH

Franklin Watts Australia
Level 17/207 Kent Street
Sydney NSW 2000

Series editor: Adrian Cole
Art Director: Jonathan Hair
Design: Simon Borrough
Picture Research: Luped

Acknowledgements:
AFP / Getty Images: 37br; Ben Birchall / PA Archive / Press Association Images: 15; Carlos Julio Martinez / AFP / Getty Images: 27t; Christian Philippe Paris / epa / Corbis: 9bl; Commonwealth of Australia 2009: 14; Cpl Ian Forsyth RLC / Crown Copyright / MOD: 18; en.wikipedia.org / wiki / File: USAF_roundel_1947: 9tl; Gregory Bergman / Alamy: 41; iStockphoto / Steve Gibson: 13c; iStockphoto / Brent Bossom: 20t; iStockphoto / naphtalina.com: 7tr; John Moore / Getty Images: 40t; Lhfgraphics / Dreamstime.com: 23t; Olivier Morin / AFP / Getty Images: 7b; Peter Macdiarmid / Getty Images: 16; Philip Wallick / Corbis: 34; Photo Courtesy of U.S. Army / SSG Adam Mancini: 6, 24t; Photo Courtesy of U.S. Army / Capt. James Reid, Combined Task Force Castle: 19b; Photo Courtesy of U.S. Army / Capt. Richard Ybarra: 25t; Photo Courtesy of U.S. Army / Werbefotografie: 16; Photo Courtesy of U.S. Army / Phil Sussman: 24b; Photo Courtesy of U.S. Army / Sgt. Jason Dangel: 40b; Photo Courtesy of U.S. Army / Spc. Monica Smith, 3rd CAB, 3rd ID Public Affairs: 25b; Photo Courtesy of U.S. Army / Spc. Richard Del Vecchio: 8; Photo Courtesy of U.S. Army / Staff Sgt. Russell Bassett Royal Navy / Crown Copyright: 9tr; Photo Courtesy of U.S. Navy / Alex Cave: 32t; Photo Courtesy of U.S. Navy / Mass Communication Specialist 1st Class Eric L. Beauregard: 32b, 33t; Photo Courtesy of U.S. Navy / Mass Communication Specialist 2nd Class David Didier: 9br; Photo Courtesy of U.S. Navy / Mass Communication Specialist 2nd Class Erik Barker: 13br; Photo Courtesy of U.S. Navy / Mass Communication Specialist 2nd Class Greg Johnson: 10; Photo Courtesy of U.S. Navy / Mass Communication Specialist 2nd Class Rafael Figueroa Medina: 30t; Photo Courtesy of U.S. Navy / Mass Communication Specialist 3rd Class Brian K. Fromal: 33b; Photo Courtesy of U.S. Navy / Mate 2nd Class Ryan Child: 17, 42cr; Photo Courtesy of U.S. Navy / Photographer's Mate 1st Class Brian McFadden: 37bl; Photo Courtesy of U.S. Navy / Photographer's Mate 3rd Class Gabriel Piper: 39b; Photo Courtesy of U.S. Navy / Photographer's Mate 3rd Class Tyler J. Clements: 39t; Rafa Salafranca / AFP / Getty Images: 21t; Reuters / Corbis: 28; Royal Navy / Crown Copyright: 29l, 29r. 30b, 31t, 31b, 42t; Shutterstock Images / Graham Taylor: 37t; Shutterstock Images / Jeremy Richards: 9cr; Shutterstock / koh sze kiat: FC; Troy GB images / Alamy: 21b; Troy GB images / Alamy: 20b; U.S. Air Force / Master Sgt Jack Braden: 35b; U.S. Air Force / Master Sgt. Andy Dunaway: 36; U.S. Air Force / Senior Airman Christopher Bush: 35t; U.S. Air Force / Staff Sgt. Shawn Weismiller: 38t; UN Photo / Evan Schneider: 19c; UN Photo / Logan Abassi: 11, 12; UN Photo / Marco Dormino : 23b; UN Photo / Sophia Paris: 38b; WO2 Fiona Stapley / Crown Copyright / MOD: 22

Contents

Fighting forces

The armed services are the military forces of a country or nation. Highly skilled and well-trained men and women defend their country using machines such as tanks, ships and aircraft.

These US soldiers from 4th Infantry Regiment are on patrol in Afghanistan.

AF FACTS

A job in the armed services is exciting, but can also be very dangerous. People can learn new skills and push themselves to the limit. In 2008, there were 20.6 million full-time troops worldwide.

The armed services operate on land, at sea and in the air, and can be sent anywhere around the world. They fight in wars, but they can also bring peace in other countries by stopping rival groups from attacking each other.

Fighter aircraft are an important part of any armed service.

In the past, armies relied on having millions of soldiers to win battles. Today, most armed services are much smaller, but the troops are more highly trained and better equipped. The Swedish Navy, for example, uses hi-tech systems on its stealth ship HMS *Helsingborg*. These allow it to share information easily with the Swedish Army and Air Force.

HMS Helsingborg is a Visby-class corvette. Its unusual shape makes it hard for enemies to detect it.

The three services

Most countries have three armed services – the army, navy and air force. Some nations also have a separate coastguard or military police force.

In the past, the army fought on land, the navy went to sea in ships and the air force flew aircraft. Today, the three armed services work together and are more of a mix. Many armies have their own helicopter units to move soldiers quickly. Marines are ground troops who use navy boats to attack from the sea.

AF FACTS

The US 101st Airborne is one of the most famous divisions in the world. They take part in air assaults (above). The division is nicknamed the 'Screaming Eagles'.

How can you tell the services apart? Each country has a different style of uniform, and each service has its own **insignia** and uniform design.

The roundel – a circular aircraft insignia – of the US Air Force.

Ground units, like those in the army or marines, have uniforms to match the surroundings. For example, they are green or brown, to blend in with forests. This makes it more difficult for the enemy to see them.

Air force pilots, like this French fighter pilot, wear special gear when in the air.

log book

inflatable collar (for use if a plane crashes at sea)

insignia

flight suit

helmet

visor

boots

A smart uniform, known as dress uniform, is worn for special occasions. These Indian soldiers are wearing dress uniform on parade.

Navy uniforms are usually blue, like the colour of the sea.

What do they do?

The main job of the armed services is to defend their country and its people. Men and women put their lives on the line so that people can live in freedom.

Air traffic controllers check the radar that scans an area over 700 kilometres (km) wide.

If your country was invaded, the armed services would try to defend you. They also help to protect you from terrorists and criminal gangs. Not all troops fight though. Many work behind the scenes in support roles, such as technicians or mechanics. In 2008, £809 billion was spent on the armed services worldwide.

Many countries send their soldiers to help the **United Nations** keep peace around the world. Sending forces to a troubled region can stop a small conflict from turning into a large war in which more people could die.

"Peace is a full-time job. The UN has over 100,000 Peacekeepers on the ground, in places others can't or won't go, doing things others can't or won't do." Actor George Clooney

Brazilian UN troops unload supplies in Haiti.

11

Different roles

Today, the armed services of many countries have different roles to play. These can include aid missions in natural disaster zones – when people are left homeless and without food after a hurricane or earthquake. They also jump into action when people need to be rescued.

These Brazilian UN peacekeepers are on duty in Haiti during a food riot after a hurricane hit the island.

When there is a hurricane or earthquake, the armed services come to the rescue. Their helicopters, boats and vehicles go to work even when the roads have been destroyed. They bring emergency food and shelter for the victims of a disaster.

In many countries, such as Canada, the USA, Denmark, Brazil and the UK, the navy and air force have search and rescue services. They rescue stranded or injured walkers or climbers around the coasts and mountains.

"Experience gained in the harsh conditions of Afghanistan has helped injured patients in the UK."
Lt Col Jeremy Henning

This search and rescue Westland Sea King is part of the Australian Navy.

AF FACTS

In 2007, four Royal Marines in Afghanistan strapped themselves to the sides of two Apache helicopters in a daring attempted rescue mission. Apache helicopters have no room for passengers.

An injured man is winched up into a helicopter from a boat in the Caribbean.

Where in the world?

The job of the armed services takes them across the globe. Some countries have large bases, or garrisons, **in other countries who want their help.**

Countries such as the UK, France and the USA have lands overseas that they want to protect. They may also have an agreement with another country to help protect them, for example Denmark currently has a naval base in Greenland.

Other countries send military forces overseas to keep the peace or patrol the seas. In 2006, Australian troops were sent to East Timor to stop riots and a rebellion by local soldiers.

These Australian troops are part of an international force on duty in East Timor.

"In the Navy you can request to serve in a variety of locations. I know many sailors that lived in Italy, Britain, Hawaii, Spain or Japan." Theodore Scott, US Navy

This British 'Jackal' crew are on patrol in Helmand, Afghanistan.

ACTION STATS

In the last 5 years, the British Armed Forces have had missions in over 30 countries, including Canada (North America), Afghanistan and Turkey (Asia), Sierra Leone (Africa), Kosovo (Europe), Brunei (Far East) and Iraq (Middle East).

Daily life

Life for people in the armed services is very different to a regular job – they can be called into action at any moment.

Fitness training in a gym is just part of daily exercise for people in the armed services.

The men and women in the armed services obey orders and follow strict rules. This helps them to stay focused when they are under pressure in a battle.

These recruits are drill training as part of their basic training.

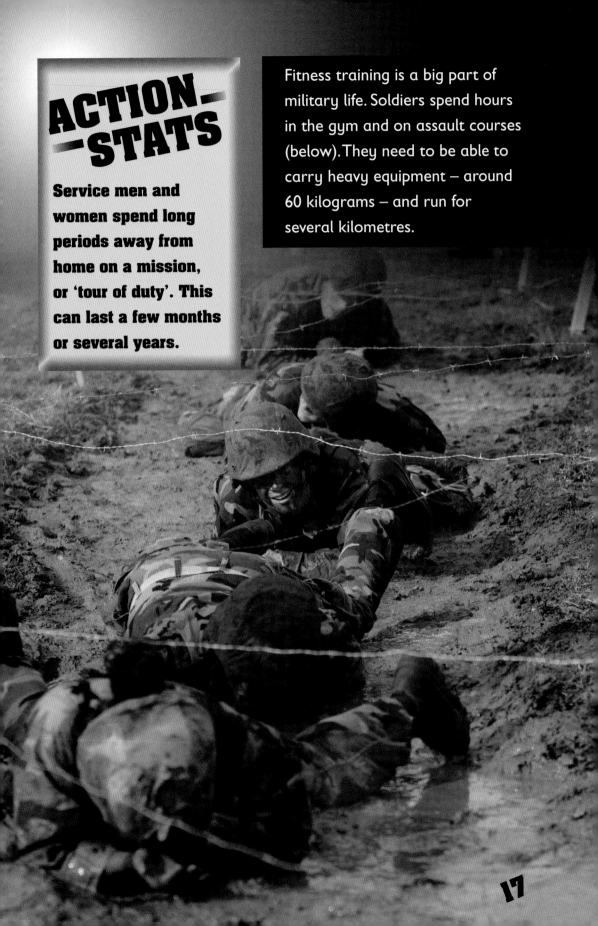

ACTION STATS

Service men and women spend long periods away from home on a mission, or 'tour of duty'. This can last a few months or several years.

Fitness training is a big part of military life. Soldiers spend hours in the gym and on assault courses (below). They need to be able to carry heavy equipment – around 60 kilograms – and run for several kilometres.

Working together

Whatever the challenge, members of the armed services rely on the friendship and support of their team. They must work together to achieve their goals – whatever they may be.

Life in the armed services is all about teamwork. Fighter pilots, tank crews and ship's gunners all rely on other people around them to do their job. While on duty they train, eat and sleep with these same people.

This Challenger 2 battle tank crew is made up of four men: the commander, gunner, loader/operator and driver.

The army, navy and air force also work together as a team. Ships can launch aircraft and provide a base for soldiers to launch an attack. Aircraft support ships or soldiers on the ground.

"You make strong friendships that last a lifetime."
Soldier in the Australian Army

Australian and US engineers work together to rebuild a bridge.

ACTION STATS

A large earthquake struck Pakistan in 2005. NATO aircraft carried 3,500 tonnes of supplies. On the ground, engineers repaired 60 km of roads.

Soldiers from Pakistan help to unload supplies.

UNITED NATIONS

Weekend warriors

Not all soldiers are full-time. Most countries have reserve **forces made up of people who have regular jobs during the week.**

Army, navy and air force reservists come from many different backgrounds. They train during their free time and provide an important back-up for the regular army and navy. Being a reservist allows people to learn new skills and keep fit.

Some reservists have support roles, including aircraft technicians.

ACTION STATS

Some countries have huge reserve armies. The top three are:
- **North Korea 4.7 million**
- **South Korea 4.5 million**
- **Vietnam 4 million**

Territorial Army (TA) units from the UK during a weekend training exercise.

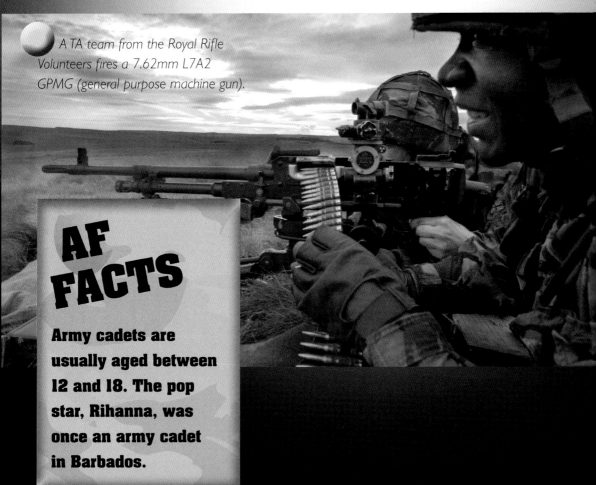

Cadet forces allow younger people to have fun while developing leadership and team skills. They can learn how to drive vehicles and how to fire weapons – although they are not expected to take part in real conflicts. All these activities prepare them for life in the armed services if they choose to join up.

"At the end of it you've done something you didn't think you could do."
Australian Air Force Officer Cadet

A cadet during training in Colombia.

A TA team from the Royal Rifle Volunteers fires a 7.62mm L7A2 GPMG (general purpose machine gun).

AF FACTS

Army cadets are usually aged between 12 and 18. The pop star, Rihanna, was once an army cadet in Barbados.

The army

The army operates on the ground. It is organised into different units that have specific skills. Officers are the leaders who give the orders, while soldiers do specific jobs such as driving a tank or operating a radio.

A member of the International Security Assistance Force (ISAF) in Afghanistan checks a 117F satellite radio.

AF FACTS

Signals **corps provide communications and IT – everything from the radios carried by a platoon, to large satellite dishes linking command centres on different continents.**

Every army unit is led by an officer. Stars, stripes and 'pips' on a uniform show his or her rank. The higher an officer's rank, the more troops he or she commands. Those shown below are from the US Army.

Private	Private First Class	Corporal	Sergent	Staff Sergent

Sergent First Class	Master Sergent	First Sergent	Sergent Major	Command Sergent Major	Sergent Major of the Army

Second Lieutenant	Major	Lieutenant Colonel	Colonel	Brigadier General	Lieutenant General	General	General of the Army

Captain

First Lieutenant

Major General

ACTION STATS

Generals command a division with thousands of troops. Colonels are in charge of 500–1,000 troops, and captains around 100. Smaller units, or squads, of 10 men are led by a sergeant.

A Sri Lankan medic examines a woman's eye. Medical teams don't just treat injured soldiers, they also assist during aid operations.

Within an army, different units, or corps, do a particular job. The infantry and tank corps fight the enemy on the ground. Engineers build bridges and keep the equipment running. The **logistics** corps organise the weapon and food supplies, while medical corps treat the wounded.

Army equipment

The army uses many types of equipment. Troops carry weapons for fighting. Vehicles carry them into battle. Soldiers also need radios, mine detectors and other equipment.

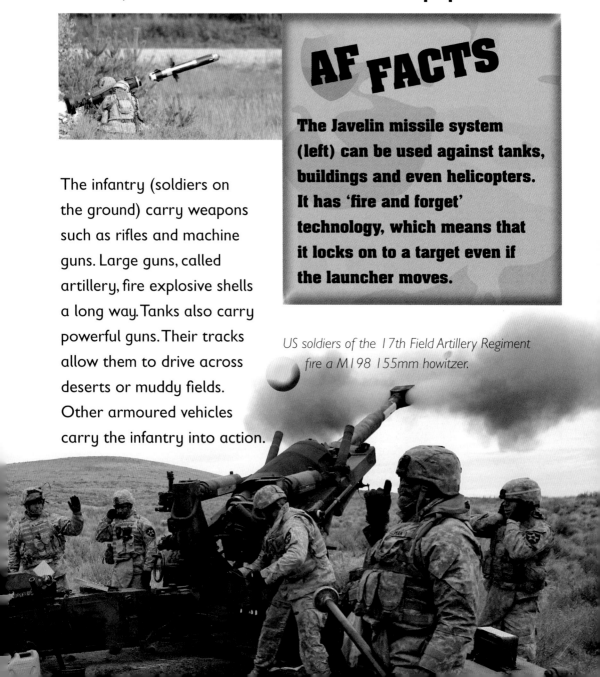

AF FACTS

The Javelin missile system (left) can be used against tanks, buildings and even helicopters. It has 'fire and forget' technology, which means that it locks on to a target even if the launcher moves.

The infantry (soldiers on the ground) carry weapons such as rifles and machine guns. Large guns, called artillery, fire explosive shells a long way. Tanks also carry powerful guns. Their tracks allow them to drive across deserts or muddy fields. Other armoured vehicles carry the infantry into action.

US soldiers of the 17th Field Artillery Regiment fire a M198 155mm howitzer.

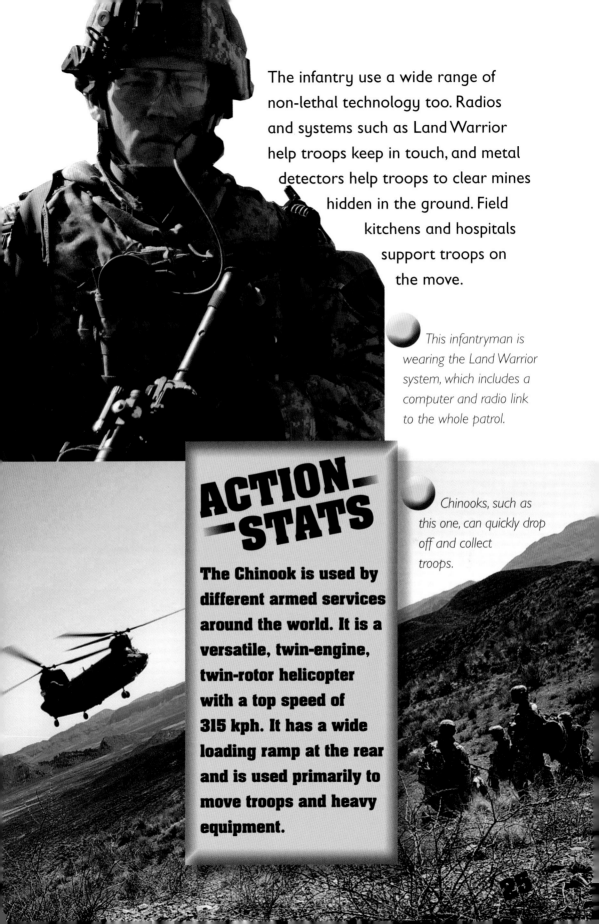

The infantry use a wide range of non-lethal technology too. Radios and systems such as Land Warrior help troops keep in touch, and metal detectors help troops to clear mines hidden in the ground. Field kitchens and hospitals support troops on the move.

This infantryman is wearing the Land Warrior system, which includes a computer and radio link to the whole patrol.

ACTION STATS

The Chinook is used by different armed services around the world. It is a versatile, twin-engine, twin-rotor helicopter with a top speed of 315 kph. It has a wide loading ramp at the rear and is used primarily to move troops and heavy equipment.

Chinooks, such as this one, can quickly drop off and collect troops.

Mission: Into battle

In June 2009, the British forces launched Operation Panther's Claw. Its aim: to attack a Taliban stronghold in the southern province of Helmand, Afghanistan.

In the first wave, over 350 soldiers were carried by 12 Chinook helicopters. Though the Taliban fought back, the force took control of several important bridges. Later, British and Danish soldiers pushed further south, capturing several towns.

This map shows the movement of the first wave in Operation Panther's Claw.

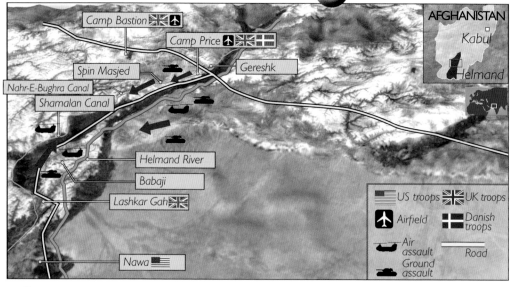

Camp Bastion

Camp Price

Spin Masjed

Gereshk

Nahr-E-Bughra Canal

Shamalan Canal

Helmand River

Babaji

Lashkar Gah

Nawa

AFGHANISTAN

Kabul

Helmand

US troops   UK troops
Airfield   Danish troops
Air assault   Road
Ground assault

A Colombian soldier walks past a burnt-out truck attacked by FARC rebels.

The armed services have often been used to rescue captured hostages. In 2008, 15 people were held prisoner by Revolutionary Armed Forces of Colombia (FARC) rebels in the mountains of Colombia. Commandos in disguise whisked them away in a helicopter.

"The helicopter almost crashed: we jumped, we screamed and we cried." Hostage Ingrid Betancourt describes the hostages' reaction when they knew they were safe.

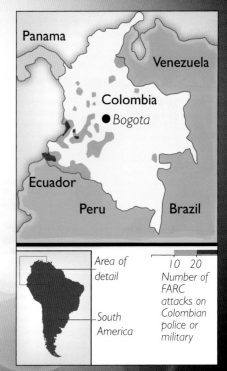

Panama

Venezuela

Colombia

● Bogota

Ecuador

Peru

Brazil

Area of detail

South America

10 20
Number of FARC attacks on Colombian police or military

The navy

The navy operates at sea using ships and aircraft. As well as defending a country from attack, it patrols the seas and supports the army.

A navy is especially important to nations with long coastlines, such as the UK, USA and China. It guards the surrounding seas and keeps trade routes open. As well as its fighting and peacekeeping duties, a navy patrols fishing grounds and oilfields.

Ships have an important part to play in the defence of many countries.

AF FACTS

Every navy has a history. The modern French Navy, under Napoleon III (1808–73), helped to build the French Empire. Napoleon used new technologies, including steam and ship armour.

There are different ranks in the navy. Admirals may command a whole fleet (see pages 30–31), while ships are commanded by a captain. Ordinary sailors are known as 'able seamen'.

The Captain stands with other naval officers above the ship's bridge.

"A lot of people do get seasick when we first sail but after a couple of days it's just a few who still get sick."
Nursing Officer Grundy, Royal Australian Navy

'Battle stations' is the highest level of alert a ship can be on. These radar operators are wearing fireproof clothing, known as anti-flash gear.

The fleet

A fleet is made up of navy ships. They are equipped with hi-tech machinery, weapons and communications gear. The ships range in size from giant aircraft carriers to small patrol boats.

USS Dwight D. Eisenhower *(aircraft carrier, top)*, USS Vicksburg *(guided-missile cruiser, centre)*, and the French FS Forbin *(destroyer, bottom)* on operations in the Arabian Sea.

Warships, such as frigates and destroyers, are also used for peacekeeping and patrol missions. **Amphibious** ships can quickly land troops and tanks. Minesweepers clear the seas of mines. Other ships are used to supply warships, map the ocean and for search and rescue missions.

Landing craft carry troops on to a beach.

ACTION STATS

Aircraft carriers are among the largest machines ever built. Over 330 metres long, they can weigh up to 100,000 tonnes. They can carry up to 85 aircraft. They also cost around £3 billion!

The crowded deck of HMS Illustrious, an Invincible class light aircraft carrier.

Nuclear-powered submarines can travel many times around the globe without needing to refuel. They can stay underwater for months at a time.

HMS Talent is a Trafalgar class hunter-killer, nuclear-powered submarine. Here, the crew are making final checks before the submarine dives under water.

Mission: Pirates!

In recent years, pirates have hijacked oil tankers and other ships off the coast of Somalia, East Africa. Ships belonging to 15 countries are working to patrol the area.

Royal Marines stop two pirate boats. They removed weapons and destroyed one boat.

In 2008, Combined Task Force 151 was sent to the region to protect ships against pirate attack. Its ships and helicopters **escort** merchant ships carrying valuable cargo, as well as hunting for pirate boats.

A visit, board, search and seizure team (VBSS) approach a pirate boat.

A VBSS team search a pirate boat for weapons.

Marines in fast patrol boats are often used to catch the pirates. Many pirates are heavily-armed, carrying rifles, machine guns and grenade-launchers.

"In the Gulf of Aden [north of Somalia], the number of attacks has gone up. But because of the presence of naval vessels, the success rate of the pirates has decreased."
Cyrus Mody, International Maritime Bureau

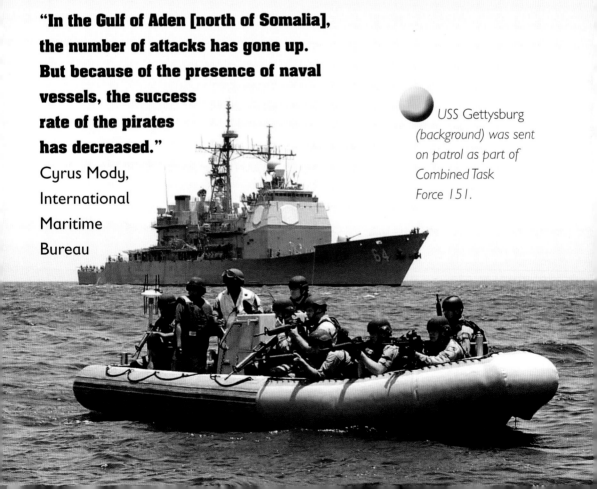

USS Gettysburg (background) was sent on patrol as part of Combined Task Force 151.

The air force

The air force operates in the skies. Planes and helicopters are used to fight enemy aircraft, as well as bomb the enemy. They also support troops on the ground.

Lockheed Martin/ Boeing's Raptor in flight.

ACTION STATS

The US-built F22 Raptor has stealth technology and is one of the best all-round fighter planes in the world. The US Air Force currently flies 139 Raptors, which have a top flying speed of 2,410 kph!

The air force also keeps the peace by flying over troublespots. Its planes and helicopters deliver supplies and carry out search and rescue missions. In an emergency, they can be used to evacuate (move) people from a danger zone.

Planes are organised into units known as squadrons. The pilots who fly the planes rely on a team of engineers, mechanics and other ground crew to keep their planes running.

Two airmen carry out important engineering checks.

"I joined because I wanted to became a pilot. It was my dream ever since I was a little kid." PFC (Private 1st Class) Charles Landeros, who works on Blackhawk helicopters in the US Army.

Pilots are briefed before every mission. There is a lot of information to take in, such as the timing, the target and the tactics.

Pilots in a briefing room prepare for a training exercise. Training instructors will also fly during this exercise to test new students.

Military aircraft

An air force has fast combat aircraft to attack targets in the air and on the ground. Larger, slower planes and helicopters are used to move troops and equipment.

The A10 Thunderbolt is nicknamed the 'Warthog'.

AF FACTS

A10 Thunderbolt II – targets tanks and other armoured vehicles
- **Guns: 1x30 mm GAU-8/A Avenger cannon, 1,174 rounds**
- **Rockets: Hydra 70, CRV7 70 mm and Zuni rockets**
- **Missiles: 2xAIM-9 Sidewinder and 8xAGM-65 Maverick**
- **Bombs: many combinations**

Fighter planes are used in air-to-air combat. Bombers and helicopters are used to attack targets on the ground. These aircraft use advanced systems to help them find their way, or navigate. Hi-tech weapons include cannons (machine guns) and missiles suited to attacks on planes, tanks, ships and buildings.

ACTION STATS

AH64 Apache Longbow – helicopter gunship (below)
- **Guns: 1 30x113 mm M230 cannon, 1,200 rounds**
- **Rockets: Hydra 70 FFAR rockets**
- **Missiles: combination of AGM-114 Hellfire, AIM-92 Stinger and AIM-9 Sidewinder**

AF FACTS

Eurofighter Typhoon – multi-role fighter (above)
- **Guns: 1x27 mm Mauser cannon**
- **Missiles: AIM-9 Sidewinder, AIM-132 ASRAAM and IRIS-T**
- **Bombs: laser-guided**

Helicopters can also be used to attack forces on the ground and to deliver troops and supplies. One of the deadliest helicopters is the AH64 Apache Longbow. It is in service in five different air forces: the US, UK, Israel, Japan and the Netherlands.

An Apache taking off (below), and a close-up of its rocket and missile systems (right).

Mission: To the rescue

A C-17 Globemaster III is loaded with aid supplies, including food and emergency equipment.

In December 2004, a giant tsunami (sea wave) struck countries around the Indian Ocean. It killed over 200,000 people and destroyed millions of homes along the coastlines of south Asia.

Within a few days, troops from around the world worked to bring in aid. Using aircraft carriers as a base, landing craft and helicopters carried emergency food and clean drinking water. Hospital ships cared for the sick and injured.

Helicopters were used to fly supplies into areas cut off because roads and railways had been destroyed.

Fresh water is wheeled across the deck of USS Abraham Lincoln.

It was a huge operation. Some 40,000 troops, sailors and aircrew took part, from more than 12 nations. The quick reaction stopped the spread of disease and saved many lives.

"Military helicopters provide a lifeline to get water, food and medical supplies to people who need them. They are hugely important."
Edward Fox, USAID

AF FACTS

The USS Abraham Lincoln produced many thousands of litres of fresh drinking water. This was pumped into plastic buckets then carried to shore by helicopters.

A helicopter lands to help a group of survivors waving a distress flag.

Changing world

The challenges faced by the armed services are always changing. Today, there are new threats from terrorists and countries who have developed nuclear weapons.

In the military, a lot of work goes into planning for the future. Some countries have created a rapid reaction force that is always ready for action. This is made up of all three services – army, navy and air force. It also includes special forces troops.

In the future, new technology may start to play an even more important role. There are already UAVs (Unmanned Aerial Vehicles) that can be remotely controlled to take photos of enemy targets or even to attack them.

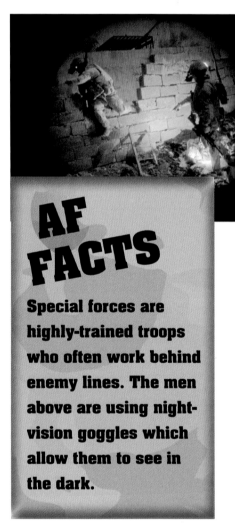

AF FACTS

Special forces are highly-trained troops who often work behind enemy lines. The men above are using night-vision goggles which allow them to see in the dark.

A UAV operator launches a RQ-7B Shadow 200. It will take up-to-date images of the surrounding area.

Many countries believe that the best way to keep the peace is to join forces with organisations such as the United Nations and NATO. By working closely with other nations, they hope to avoid conflict.

The USS Oriskany was taken out of service in 2006. The former aircraft carrier was sunk off the Florida coast to form a reef for sealife.

Fast facts

- Each year, over £20 billion is spent on the armed services in the UK, employing over 300,000 people.

- The UK, India and Canada still have cavalry regiments – soldiers do guard duties on horseback. But they fight in tanks or other armoured vehicles.

- The USA has the world's largest air force, with over 6,000 planes and over 300,000 men and woman on active duty.

- A Tristar fuel-tanker refuels other planes while they are still flying. It carries over 85,000 litres of fuel, enough for an average car to drive around the world three times.

- A navy often has a floating hospital so that members of the armed services can get the best medical care close to where they are fighting.

- Some countries, including Iceland, Costa Rica and Morocco, have no army.

Glossary

Amphibious – a vehicle or force that operates on both land and water.

Cadet – a military trainee.

Engineers – the part of the armed services that looks after all the equipment, from helicopters to rifles. Some engineers build bridges and make maps.

Escort – to go along with and protect someone or something.

Garrison – a military base.

Hijack – to take by force.

Insignia – badges, for example, such as stripes worn to show rank.

Logistics – moving and storing supplies such as food or equipment.

NATO – a military organisation. Members include the USA, UK, Canada, France and Germany.

Natural disaster – the result of natural events, such as a tsunami or earthquake.

Nuclear-powered – submarines and ships with an engine driven by a nuclear reactor.

Peacekeepers – military forces used to keep the peace, often by keeping two enemy forces apart.

Platoon – a small group of soldiers.

Radar – a device that tracks planes and ships using radio waves.

Reserve – part-time armed forces that are used in an emergency.

Signals – military communications such as radios, which allow the armed forces to share information.

Stealth technology – smooth design to help hide from enemy radar.

United Nations – an organisation created in 1949 to promote international peace.

Weapons of mass destruction – weapons that cause massive damage and loss of life, such as nuclear bombs.

Websites

www.army.mod.uk

This is the website of the British Army, giving information about its history, its missions and its equipment.

www.army.mil

The US Army website, with videos and pictures of US troops in action and talking about their jobs.

www.royalnavy.mod.uk

The website of the British Royal Navy, featuring facts, pictures and videos about its history, its operations and the different jobs in the Navy.

www.navy.mil

Website of the US Navy, with hundreds of photos of ships and crews at work.

www.raf.mod.uk

The on-line home of the British Royal Air Force (RAF), including information about its history, role and equipment.

www.defence.gov.au/Army

All about the Australian Army, with details about the history, equipment and today's missions. Also includes an interactive section with photos and videos.

www.un.org/Depts/dpko/dpko

Part of the United Nations website focusing on peacekeeping operations. It includes information about current operations, photos and webcasts.

www.defense.gouv.fr/marine

The website of the French Navy (which can be read in French, English or Spanish). It includes up-to-date news articles and a media gallery with virtual tours.

www.iwm.org.uk

The website of the Imperial War Museum offers a look at how armed conflict has shaped our lives.

www.mod.uk/DefenceInternet/Home

Home page of the British Ministry of Defence website, featuring news on all three armed services and videos of military equipment in action.

www.history.army.mil

Website of the US Army Center of Military History that includes photos of past conflicts and a searchable poster gallery.

Index